ALPHABETIC INDEXING

6th Edition

MODEL CURRICULUM
FOR OFFICE CAREERS

Mearl R. Guthrie, Professor Emeritus
Business Education Department
Bowling Green State University
Bowling Green, Ohio

Carolyn V. Norwood
Business Division
Essex County College
Newark, New Jersey

JOIN US ON THE INTERNET
WWW: http://www.thomson.com
EMAIL: findit@kiosk.thomson.com   A service of I(T)P®

South-Western Educational Publishing
an International Thomson Publishing company I(T)P®

Cincinnati • Albany, NY • Belmont, CA • Bonn • Boston • Detroit • Johannesburg • London • Madrid
Melbourne • Mexico City • New York • Paris • Singapore • Tokyo • Toronto • Washington

Project Manager: Marilyn Hornsby
Editor: Michelle Kunkler and Kimberlee Kusnerak
Production Coordinator: Jane Congdon
Manufacturing Coordinator: Carol Chase
Marketing Manager: Tim Gleim
Publishing Team Leader: Karen Schmohe
Art & Design Coordinator: Michelle Kunkler
Internal Design: Kathy Heming
Cover Design: Laura Brown
Production Services: Kathy Heming

■ TABLE OF CONTENTS ■

■ PREFACE ■

ALPHABETIC INDEXING, Sixth Edition, is a thorough instruction program for alphabetic indexing rules and procedures. Quick and easy access to records is very important in business operations. Only 15 to 20 hours are necessary to learn and apply the 14 indexing rules. This learner-oriented text-workbook may be used in high schools, vocational schools, adult education programs, colleges, and universities.

ALPHABETIC INDEXING, Sixth Edition, has been totally revised. The 14 new indexing rules are in compliance with the filing standards recommended by the Association of Records Managers and Administrators, Inc. (ARMA). ARMA is the professional organization responsible for establishing standards in the records management field. The new rules in the Sixth Edition provide for simplicity and consistency in filing. Automated records storage is made easier through the use of these simplified rules.

ALPHABETIC INDEXING, Sixth Edition, is organized into six parts. Part I — Alphabetic Indexing Rules 1-4 covers order of indexing units, minor words and symbols in business names, punctuation and possessives, and single letters and abbreviations. Part II — Alphabetic Indexing Rules 5-8 covers titles and suffixes, married women, articles and particles, and identical names. Part III — Alphabetic Indexing Rules 9-12 covers numbers in business names, organizations and institutions, separated single words, and hyphenated names. Part IV — Alphabetic Indexing Rules 13-14 covers compound names and government names. Part V — Cross-Referencing provides a listing of the types of names that need to be cross-referenced with examples of the correct way to cross-reference each type of name. Part VI — Other Filing Methods introduces subject, numeric, and geographic filing. A review of the 14 indexing rules concludes the Sixth Edition.

In the new Sixth Edition, learning objectives are presented at the beginning of each part. Each rule statement is followed by a list of examples applying that rule. Twenty-one exercises that provide opportunities for indexing, coding, and filing are placed at the ends of the parts. Eight applications that provide for indexing, coding, and filing of cards are included. A glossary of filing terms is given on page 1. A list of two-letter state abbreviations is printed on the inside of the front cover.

The Teacher's Manual shows the correct indexing, coding, and filing order of all exercises and applications. Comprehensive tests and their answers for the alphabetic, subject, numeric, and geographic methods are included. Transparency masters for the review of the 14 indexing rules are in the new Sixth Edition Manual.

The new ALPHABETIC INDEXING, Sixth Edition, can be used in conjunction with MICROFILE II *A Database Filing Program,* by Joseph S. Fosegan, South-Western Educational Publishing, 1996. A small computer indicates the exercises in ALPHABETIC INDEXING that can be used with MICROFILE II.

Filing is a very simple operation as long as everyone is playing by the same rules. The Sixth Edition indexing rules are recommended for all types of businesses.

■ PART I ~ ALPHABETIC INDEXING RULES 1-4 ■

Learning Objectives

After completing Part I, you will be able to:

1. Index and alphabetize common personal names, including those containing possessives.
2. Index and alphabetize common business names, including those containing prepositions, conjunctions, symbols, articles, punctuation, possessives, single letters, abbreviations, and acronyms.

Definitions of Terms

Filing
The systematic and orderly arrangement and storage of records (cards, letters, invoices, statements, catalogs, blueprints, newspapers, and other office and personal records) for future reference.

Alphabetizing
The arrangement of single letters and words in dictionary order from A to Z.

Filing Segment
The name, subject, number, or location by which a record is filed.

Indexing
The mental process of dividing filing segments into indexing units.

Indexing Unit
A part of a filing segment that is used in indexing.

Key Unit
The first indexing unit of the filing segment.

Coding
The process of marking the indexing units to indicate the order in which those units are to be considered in filing.

Indexing Order
The order in which a name is written for indexing purposes; that is, the order with the key indexing unit written first, the second indexing unit written second, and so on.

Alphabetic Filing Order
The final alphabetic arrangement of the filing segments.

Personal Name
The legal name of a person, whether that name stands alone or is part of a business name.

Given Name
The first name or initial of a person and the middle name or initial, if any.

Surname
The last name of a person.

Full Name
The surname and at least one given name or initial of a person.

Business Name
The official name of a company, a corporation, a partnership (firm), an organization, or an association.

Rule 1 – Order of Indexing Units

A. Personal Names. Index full personal names in this order: (1) the surname (last name) is the key unit, (2) the given name (first name) or initial is the second unit, and (3) the middle name or initial is the third unit. Unusual or obscure names are indexed in the same manner. If it is not possible to determine the surname in a name, consider the last name as the surname. Cross-reference unusual or obscure names by using the first written name as the key unit.

Study the following examples. In the examples, underlines indicate the letters in the units that determine the alphabetic sequence.

	ALPHABETIC FILING ORDER		
NAME	KEY UNIT	UNIT 2	UNIT 3
1. Allen N. Colson	Colson	Allen	N
2. Arthur Colson	Colson	Arthur	
3. Angelina Cubero	Cubero	Angelina	
4. Angelina V. Cubero	Cubero	Angelina	V
5. Bhikku Pai	Pai	Bhikku	
6. W. James Pollard	Pollard	W	James
7. Wayne Pollard	Pollard	Wayne	
8. Victoria A. Ray	Ray	Victoria	A
9. Victoria A. Raye	Raye	Victoria	A
10. Willadean Solon	Solon	Willadean	
11. William Solon	Solon	William	
12. Hoo Soo	Soo	Hoo	

B. Business Names. Index business names as they are written using letterheads or trademarks as guides. If a business name contains a personal name, index the name in the order it is written. Newspapers and periodicals are indexed as written. For newspapers and periodicals having identical names that do not include the city name, consider the city name as the last indexing unit. If necessary, the state name may follow the city name.

Study the following examples.

	ALPHABETIC FILING ORDER		
NAME	KEY UNIT	UNIT 2	UNIT 3
1. Golden Dragon Kitchen	Golden	Dragon	Kitchen
2. Hillside Times	Hillside	Times	
3. Linda Perrone Fashions	Linda	Perrone	Fashions
4. Martin Schwartz Associates	Martin	Schwartz	Associates
5. Morning News (Columbia)	Morning	News	Columbia
6. Morning News (Florence)	Morning	News	Florence
7. Robert Lawrence Realtors	Robert	Lawrence	Realtors
8. Rosado Delgado Boutique	Rosado	Delgado	Boutique
9. Stevens Credit Company	Stevens	Credit	Company
10. Su Cheng Restaurant	Su	Cheng	Restaurant

C. Coding Directions. Coding is the marking or underlining of indexing units. In the examples below, you will index and code the names by (1) marking off the units with diagonal lines, (2) underlining the first (key) unit, and (3) numbering the remaining units by writing above them the numbers that indicate their correct order. (The first two names below are given as examples.)

State/Farm/Insurance   Star Sports Incorporated

A./Carol/Skinner   Walter J. Stavisky

Star Gazzette   O. J. Singleton

Name (Indexing Order)   Date

Instructions. Study pages 1 and 2 before completing this exercise.

1. Index and code each of the names listed below by (a) marking off the units with diagonal lines, (b) underlining the first (key) unit, and (c) numbering the remaining units by writing above them the numbers that indicate their correct order. (The first two names below are given as examples.)

2. Indicate the correct filing order of these names by writing the filing-order number (1, 2, 3, etc.) on the blank line in front of each name. (Write these filing order numbers in pencil so you can easily make changes to achieve the correct filing order.)

3. Write the names in correct alphabetic filing order in the space provided. Write names and initials in each column close to the vertical lines. Keep your work neat and your writing small.

<table>
<tr><td>___6___ William/<u>Martin</u></td><td>_____ Marian Martinez</td></tr>
<tr><td>___4___ Edward/D./<u>Clark</u></td><td>_____ Jason Mellito</td></tr>
<tr><td>_____ Maria A. Martinez</td><td>_____ James Thomas Mills</td></tr>
<tr><td>_____ Robert Chang</td><td>_____ Edna D. Clark</td></tr>
<tr><td>_____ E. David Parks</td><td>_____ Hassan Muhammad</td></tr>
<tr><td>_____ J. R. Colbert</td><td>_____ Derek E. Parks</td></tr>
<tr><td>_____ Stephen Miller</td><td>_____ Roberta E. Chang</td></tr>
<tr><td>_____ Joan Mellito</td><td>_____ Stephanie Miller</td></tr>
</table>

ALPHABETIC FILING ORDER

	KEY UNIT	UNIT 2	UNIT 3
1.			
2.			
3.			
4.	Clark	Edward	D
5.			
6.	Martin	William	
7.			
8.			
9.			
10.			
11.			
12.			
13.			
14.			
15.			
16.			

Name (Indexing Order)   Date

Instructions. Study pages 1 and 2 before completing this exercise.

1. Index and code each of the names listed below by (a) marking off the units with diagonal lines, (b) underlining the first (key) unit, and (c) numbering the remaining units by writing above them the numbers that indicate their correct order. (The first two names below are given as examples.)

2. Indicate the correct filing order of these names by writing the filing-order number (1, 2, 3, etc.) on the blank line in front of each name. (Write these filing-order numbers in pencil so you can easily make changes to achieve the correct filing order.)

3. Write the names in correct alphabetic filing order in the space provided. Write names and initials in each column close to the vertical lines. Keep your work neat and your writing small.

<table>
<tr><td>__2__ <u>Bernard</u>/Schuman/Clothiers ^{2 3}</td><td>_____ Daily Messenger (Irvington)</td></tr>
<tr><td>__11__ <u>Dominico</u>/Tours ²</td><td>_____ Bernardsville Shoe Outlet</td></tr>
<tr><td>_____ Butler Brothers Construction</td><td>_____ David Lucas Realtors</td></tr>
<tr><td>_____ Daily Messenger (Maplewood)</td><td>_____ Davidson Transportation Company</td></tr>
<tr><td>_____ Benjamin Chu Home Repairs</td><td>_____ Paskas Furniture Company</td></tr>
<tr><td>_____ Diana Diaz Catering Service</td><td>_____ Menorah Chapels Incorporated</td></tr>
<tr><td>_____ Star Ledger</td><td>_____ Lola Daniels Boutique</td></tr>
<tr><td>_____ Melody Record Shops</td><td>_____ Denise Parks Novelty Shop</td></tr>
</table>

ALPHABETIC FILING ORDER

	KEY UNIT	UNIT 2	UNIT 3	UNIT 4
1.				
2.	Bernard	Schuman	Clothiers	
3.				
4.				
5.				
6.				
7.				
8.				
9.				
10.				
11.	Dominico	Tours		
12.				
13.				
14.				
15.				
16.				

Rule 2 – Minor Words and Symbols in Business Names

Each word in a business name is considered a separate indexing unit. Prepositions, conjunctions, symbols, and articles are included; symbols (&, ¢, $, #, %) are considered as spelled in full (and, Cent, Dollar, Number, Percent). All spelled-out symbols except "and" begin with a capital letter.

When the word "The" appears as the first word of a business name, it is considered the last indexing unit.

Study the following examples. In the examples, underlines indicate the letters in the units that determine the alphabetic sequence.

		ALPHABETIC FILING ORDER			
NAME	KEY UNIT	UNIT 2	UNIT 3	UNIT 4	UNIT 5
1. A Pleasant Day Nursery School	A	Pleasant	Day	Nursery	School
2. Abraham & Strauss Stores	Abraham	and	Strauss	Stores	
3. Abraham Clark Motors	Abraham	Clark	Motors		
4. Bridals By Lisa	Bridals	By	Lisa		
5. $s for Shopping	Dollars	for	Shopping		
6. In Step Podiatry	In	Step	Podiatry		
7. Inn of the Three Knights	Inn	of	the	Three	Knights
8. Instant Alarm Service	Instant	Alarm	Service		
9. Inway Independent Freight	Inway	Independent	Freight		
10. One Cut Above	One	Cut	Above		
11. One Stop Market	One	Stop	Market		
12. Touch of Elegance Salon	Touch	Of	Elegance	Salon	
13. The Town & Country Shop	Town	and	Country	Shop	The
14. The Town & Country Store	Town	and	Country	Store	The
15. Tsao Oriental Fabrics	Tsao	Oriental	Fabrics		
16. Your Big % Discounter	Your	Big	Percent	Discounter	

Rule 3 – Punctuation and Possessives

Disregard all punctuation when indexing personal and business names. Commas, periods, hyphens, and apostrophes are ignored; names are indexed as written. (For example, Rogers' Brothers Electronics would be filed before Roger's Record Shop.)

Study the following examples.

		ALPHABETIC FILING ORDER			
NAME	KEY UNIT	UNIT 2	UNIT 3	UNIT 4	UNIT 5
1. Jack & Jill Wedding Apparel	Jack	and	Jill	Wedding	Apparel
2. Jacks Amoco Service Station	Jacks	Amoco	Service	Station	
3. Jacks' Heating Systems	Jacks	Heating	Systems		
4. Jack's House of Beauty	Jacks	House	of	Beauty	
5. Robert E. Jacks	Jacks	Robert	E		
6. Jacks, Roberts & Lopez	Jacks	Roberts	and	Lopez	
7. Theresa Jacks	Jacks	Theresa			
8. Jacks' Unistop Haircutters	Jacks	Unistop	Haircutters		

Rule 4 – Single Letters and Abbreviations

A. Personal Names. Initials in personal names are separate indexing units. Abbreviations of personal names (Wm., Jos., Thos.) and brief personal names or nicknames (Liz, Bill) are indexed as they are written.

B. Business Names. Index single letters in business names as they are written. If there is a space between single letters, index each letter as a separate unit. An acronym (a word formed from the first, or first few, letters of several words) is indexed as one unit. Abbreviations are indexed as one unit regardless of punctuation or spacing (AAA, Y M C A, Y.W.C.A.). Radio and television station call letters are indexed as one word. Cross-reference spelled-out names to their acronyms or abbreviations if necessary. For example: National Broadcasting Company SEE NBC.

Study the following examples.

	ALPHABETIC FILING ORDER			
NAME	KEY UNIT	UNIT 2	UNIT 3	UNIT 4
1. A & S Stores	A	and	S	Stores
2. A. Jan Ross Enterprises	A	Jan	Ross	Enterprises
3. AAT Communications	AAT	Communications		
4. William T. Nelson	Nelson	William	T	
5. Wm. T. Nelson	Nelson	Wm	T	
6. J. R. Nudelman	Nudelman	J	R	
7. Liz Porcelli	Porcelli	Liz		
8. Liz A. Porcelli	Porcelli	Liz	A	
9. Toni Vazquez	Vazquez	Toni		
10. VIP Honda Sport Center	VIP	Honda	Sport	Center
11. WOR Television Station	WOR	Television	Station	

Name (Indexing Order)   Date

Instructions. Study pages 1 through 6 before completing this exercise.

1. Index and code each of the names listed below by (a) marking off the units with diagonal lines, (b) underlining the first (key) unit, and (c) numbering the remaining units by writing above them the numbers that indicate their correct order. (The first two names below are given as examples.)

2. Indicate the correct filing order of these names by writing the filing-order number (1, 2, 3, etc.) on the blank line in front of each name. (Write these filing-order numbers in pencil so you can easily make changes to achieve the correct filing order.)

3. Write the names in correct alphabetic filing order in the space provided. Write names and initials in each column close to the vertical lines. Keep your work neat and your writing small.

5 <u>Isuzu</u>/of/Hillside *(2, 3)*	_____ Nam-It Engraving Company
7 Thomas/<u>Iverson</u> *(2)*	_____ ITT Industrial Credit Company
_____ Jackie & Jill Studios	_____ Izguierdo's Bakery
_____ Margaret Jackson	_____ Margaret A. Jackson
_____ Tom Iverson	_____ Jackson's Funeral Home
_____ Imperial Cab Company	_____ Jade Pagoda Chinese Restaurant
_____ The Ink Well	_____ Wong Chu
_____ Pedro Izguierdo	_____ In Town Motor Lodge

ALPHABETIC FILING ORDER

	KEY UNIT	UNIT 2	UNIT 3	UNIT 4
1.				
2.				
3.				
4.				
5.	Isuzu	of	Hillside	
6.				
7.	Iverson	Thomas		
8.				
9.				
10.				
11.				
12.				
13.				
14.				
15.				
16.				

Instructions. Study pages 1 through 6 before completing this exercise.

1. Index and code each of the names listed below by (a) marking off the units with diagonal lines, (b) underlining the first (key) unit, and (c) numbering the remaining units by writing above them the numbers that indicate their correct order. (The first two names below are given as examples.)
2. Indicate the correct filing order of these names by writing the filing-order number (1, 2, 3, etc.) on the blank line in front of each name. (Write these filing-order numbers in pencil so you can easily make changes to achieve the correct filing order.)
3. Write the names in correct alphabetic filing order in the space provided.

__2__	J̲/A./Brown/Carpeting		_____	Juan Perez
__3__	J̲B̲M̲/Television/Service		_____	Nita Perkins
_____	Park's Radiology Group		_____	L. E. Parks
_____	Parkside Inn		_____	Pick A Flick Video
_____	Parks' Janitorial Services		_____	Pan-Urban Travel Agency
_____	Park & Ride		_____	The Pipe Shop
_____	Parkway Village Apartments		_____	Wei Pu
_____	Annette Pecorella		_____	Ice N Air Equipment

ALPHABETIC FILING ORDER

	KEY UNIT	UNIT 2	UNIT 3	UNIT 4
1.				
2.	J	A	Brown	Carpeting
3.	JBM	Television	Service	
4.				
5.				
6.				
7.				
8.				
9.				
10.				
11.				
12.				
13.				
14.				
15.				
16.				

In most business offices, it is frequently necessary to file cards or business papers in alphabetic order. The applications at the end of each part in ALPHABETIC INDEXING have been designed to give you a realistic filing practice.

Instructions. Use the following procedure in completing Application 1 (cards 101-120): (1) tear out the 20 file cards on pages 9 and 11, (2) code each name on the Application 1 file cards in the manner described on page 10, (3) arrange the cards in proper alphabetic filing order, (4) list the numeric order of your stack of cards on a separate sheet of paper, and (5) check the alphabetic arrangement (numeric order) with your teacher.

101

All-Temp Refrigeration Service

750 Elmhurst Circle

Orlando, FL 32810-5171

102

House of Records

384 Tewkesbury Place, NW

Washington, DC 20012-3219

103

Robt. Fitzgerald

620 Amherst Road

Columbia, MO 65211-4812

104

E. J. Perez

5555 Los Robles Street

Rio Piedras, PR 00927-2820

105

Regina Agency Incorporated

2330 Girard Avenue

Philadelphia, PA 19130-1637

106

Laverne Tamburino

20 Cold Spring Road

Hatfield, AR 71945-1123

107

Deborah Hirshfeld

2500 Lakewood Drive

Louisville, KY 40292-1438

108

Honda Motorcycles

897 Winchester Avenue

Colorado Springs, CO 80904-1356

109

Sung Hong

218 Collins Boulevard

La Grande, OR 97850-1754

110

Arthur Fowler

4418 Woodland Avenue

Belt, MT 59412-2397

Code all of the cards in the application activities in the following manner: (l) mark off the units with diagonal lines, (2) underline the key unit, and (3) number the remaining units by writing above them the numbers that indicate their correct order.

Complete Application 2 (cards 201-220) on pages 10 and 12. Follow the same procedures outlined for the Application 1 cards.

201

Quick-Chek Food Stores

1121 Wilburn Drive

Rockville, MD 20852-1432

202

Pulaski's Meat Products

320 Broad Street

Council Bluffs, IA 51501-1667

203

House of Glamour

15 Tangerine Avenue

Los Altos, CA 94023-1705

204

The Daily Mirror

One Park Avenue

Wilmington, DE 19804-1430

205

Pulaski Uniform Supply

17 Wilcox Parkway

Ypsilanti, MI 48197-2427

206

Overlook Hospital

82 Roseway Court

Honolulu, HI 96817-2354

207

Phillip C. Ritter

388 Chestnut Street

Virginia Beach, VA 23454-1122

208

Sylvia Pugliese

255 Central Avenue

Austin, TX 78745-1555

209

A. B. Griffith Laboratories

916 Seventh Avenue

Madison, WI 53714-1762

210

Jos. Quinn

1517 Rocky Way Drive

Florence, SC 29501-1956

111

Herald Post News

398 Kennedy Boulevard

New Haven, CT 06511-8241

116

E. Jose Perez

694 Cherry Lane

Lawrenceville, GA 30246-1293

112

Smith, Klein & James Contractors

919 Bloomfield Avenue

Tucson, AZ 85703-6502

117

Art Fowler

38 Bell Boulevard

Jackson, MS 39213-2587

113

AAA Discount Store

888 E. 34 Street

Ketchikan, AK 99901-7081

118

D. Hirshfeld Realtors

277 Needle Point Lane

Logan, UT 84321-1965

114

The Cabinet Makers

11 S. 17 Street

Ypsilanti, MI 48197-1587

119

P'S & Q's

10 Sandy Hollow Road

Cheyenne, WY 82001-3355

115

Hit or Miss

72-40 E. 52 Avenue

Las Cruces, NM 88003-9613

120

Peggy's Florist

605 Riverside Drive

Newark, NJ 07104-4410

12

APPLICATION 2
Rules 1-4

211

Yongok Choi

32 Race Street

Philadelphia, PA 19110-1944

212

WBLS Radio Station

841 Fifth Avenue

Spokane, WA 99207-1389

213

A.D.T. Security Systems

288 Fairfield Avenue

Weatherford, OK 73096-1987

214

Acme Brokerage Incorporated

354 West 35 Street

Reno, NV 89512-1321

215

Y. Charles Abernathy

1111 Brookgreen Drive

Middlebury, VT 05753-1457

216

Levine, Cruz & Davis, Esquires

185 Eppirt Street

East Providence, RI 02914-1598

217

Quick Printing & Copying

442 Broadway

Nashville, TN 37209-1313

218

Joe T. Quinn

700 Poplar Avenue

Institute, WV 25112-1841

219

Phillipa Ritter

6623 Columbus Avenue

Charlotte, NC 28211-1497

220

Yolanda Abernathy

515 S. Elm Drive

Columbus, OH 43221-4045

■ PART II ~ ALPHABETIC INDEXING RULES 5-8 ■

Learning Objectives

After completing Part II, you will be able to:

1. Index and alphabetize personal and business names with titles and suffixes.
2. Index and alphabetize married women's names.
3. Index and alphabetize names with articles and particles (prefixes).
4. Index and alphabetize identical personal and business names.

Rule 5 – Titles and Suffixes

A. Personal Names. A personal or professional title before a name (Miss, Mr., Mrs., Ms., Dr., Prof.) is the last indexing unit. If a seniority suffix is required for identification, it is considered the last indexing unit in abbreviated form, with numeric (II, III) filed before alphabetic suffixes (Jr., Sr.). When professional suffixes (D.D.S., M.D., CRM, Mayor) are required for identification, they are considered the last units and filed alphabetically as written. If a name contains both a title and a suffix, the title is the last unit. Royal and religious titles followed by either a given name or a surname only (Father Leo) are indexed and filed as written. When all units of identical names, including titles and suffixes, have been compared and there are no differences, filing order is determined by the addresses.

Titles and suffixes are indexed as written without punctuation. For example: Jr., Dr., Maj., Major are indexed as Jr, Dr, Maj, Major.

Study the following examples.

		ALPHABETIC FILING ORDER		
NAME	**KEY UNIT**	**UNIT 2**	**UNIT 3**	**UNIT 4**
1. Brother Joseph	Brother	Joseph		
2. Amy E. Brown	Brown	Amy	E	
3. Arthur Brown	Brown	Arthur		
4. Miss Chris P. Majoros	Majoros	Chris	P	Miss
5. Mrs. Chris P. Majoros	Majoros	Chris	P	Mrs
6. Ms. Chris P. Majoros	Majoros	Chris	P	Ms
7. Major Joseph Maynes	Maynes	Joseph	Major	
8. Mayor Josephine Maynes	Maynes	Josephine	Mayor	
9. William J. Mayor II	Mayor	William	J	II
10. William J. Mayor III	Mayor	William	J	III
11. William J. Mayor, Jr.	Mayor	William	J	Jr
12. Rev. William J. Mayor	Mayor	William	J	Rev
13. William J. Mayor, Sr.	Mayor	William	J	Sr
14. Virginia A. Mays, DDS	Mays	Virginia	A	DDS
15. Dr. Virginia A. Mays	Mays	Virginia	A	Dr
16. Constance Y. Wong	Wong	Constance	Y	

B. Business Names. Titles in business names are filed as written. See Rules 1 and 2.

Study the following examples.

NAME	KEY UNIT	ALPHABETIC FILING ORDER		
		UNIT 2	UNIT 3	UNIT 4
1. DOC Optical Centers	DOC	Optical	Centers	
2. Doctor Music	Doctor	Music		
3. Dr. Henry Stanley Building	Dr	Henry	Stanley	Building
4. Dr. Scholl's Shoe Co.	Dr	Scholls	Shoe	Co
5. Major Cox Corporation	Major	Cox	Corporation	
6. Majors Shoe Store	Majors	Shoe	Store	
7. Mayor Jewelry Co.	Mayor	Jewelry	Co	
8. Mayor's Clothing	Mayors	Clothing		
9. Miss Kitty's Salon	Miss	Kittys	Salon	
10. Mister George Beauty Salon	Mister	George	Beauty	Salon
11. Mr. D's Lounge	Mr	Ds	Lounge	
12. Mrs. D's Delivery Service	Mrs	Ds	Delivery	Service
13. Prince Frederick Stores	Prince	Frederick	Stores	
14. Prince's Food Store	Princes	Food	Store	
15. Princess Exercise Room	Princess	Exercise	Room	
16. Sisters Health Foods	Sisters	Health	Foods	

Rule 6 – Married Women

A married woman's name is filed as she writes it. It is indexed according to Rule 1. If more than one form of a name is known, the alternate name may be cross-referenced.

A married woman's name in a business name is indexed as written and follows Rules 1B and 5B.

Study the following examples.

NAME	KEY UNIT	ALPHABETIC FILING ORDER		
		UNIT 2	UNIT 3	UNIT 4
1. Mrs. Judy Johnson *(Mrs. James T. Johnson)	Johnson	Judy	Mrs	
2. Mrs. Leeann Johnson	Johnson	Leeann	Mrs	
3. Mrs. Lisa Norman Johnson	Johnson	Lisa	Norman	Mrs
4. Mrs. Lois Johnson	Johnson	Lois	Mrs	
5. Ms. Lonnetta Wilson Johnson *(Mrs. Samuel Johnson) *(Mrs. Lonnetta Johnson)	Johnson	Lonnetta	Wilson	Ms
6. Mrs. Loretta Wilson Johnson *(Mrs. Loretta Wilson)	Johnson	Loretta	Wilson	Mrs
7. Mrs. Marc C. Johnson *(Mrs. Maggie A. Johnson)	Johnson	Marc	C	Mrs
8. Mrs. Stovers Candy	Mrs	Stovers	Candy	
9. Mrs. Velez Travel Agency	Mrs	Velez	Travel	Agency
10. Mrs. Chien Yung	Yung	Chien	Mrs	

*A cross-reference would be prepared for this alternate name.

Name (Indexing Order)   Date

Instructions. Study pages 13 and 14 before completing this exercise. Proceed as you did with previous indexing exercises. (1) Index and code each of the names in the list below. (2) Write the correct filing-order number in front of each name. (3) Write the names in correct alphabetic filing order in the space provided.

_____ Mr. Travel Inc.

_____ Col. Norman D. Cummings

_____ Ernest Mosakowski, Ph.D.

_____ World Wide Travel Agency

_____ Raymond B. Klear

_____ Mr. Martin J. Mrowzinski

_____ Johnson & Johnson

_____ Miss Nancy O. Hernandez

_____ Mrs. Clean Supplies

_____ Mrs. Johnnie Mae Johnson

_____ The Colonel's Inn

_____ Mrs. Theda M. Colson

_____ YKK Zipper Co.

_____ Ms. Kelly's Kleaners

_____ Worldwide Car Service, Inc.

_____ Venetia Yung

ALPHABETIC FILING ORDER

	KEY UNIT	UNIT 2	UNIT 3	UNIT 4
1.				
2.				
3.				
4.				
5.				
6.				
7.				
8.				
9.				
10.				
11.				
12.				
13.				
14.				
15.				
16.				

Name (Indexing Order)   Date

Instructions. Study pages 13 and 14 before completing this exercise. Proceed as you did with previous indexing exercises. (1) Index and code each of the names in the list below. (2) Write the correct filing-order number in front of each name. (3) Write the names in correct alphabetic filing order in the space provided.

_____ Athena Chang

_____ Lady Jane's Modeling Agency

_____ Jas. C. Smith, Sr.

_____ Betty Rumpf Interiors, Inc.

_____ Miss Jane Smith

_____ J. R. Smith II

_____ Runner Equipment Co.

_____ Lady Essex Appliances

_____ Ms. Jennie Smith

_____ Jane Wolff Smith

_____ Frank H. Rumpf Co.

_____ Frank C. Rumpf, Atty.

_____ Jas. C. Smith, Jr.

_____ Dr. Mark Tsuang

_____ Rumpus Room Bowling Lanes

_____ J. R. Smith III

ALPHABETIC FILING ORDER

	KEY UNIT	UNIT 2	UNIT 3	UNIT 4
1.				
2.				
3.				
4.				
5.				
6.				
7.				
8.				
9.				
10.				
11.				
12.				
13.				
14.				
15.				
16.				

Rule 7 – Articles and Particles

Combine an article or particle in a personal or business name with the part of the name following it to form a single indexing unit. The indexing order is not affected by spaces or punctuation between a prefix and the rest of the name. Disregard the spaces and punctuation when indexing. Examples of articles and particles are: a la, D', Da, De, Del, De la, Della, Den, Des, Di, Dos, Du, El, Fitz, Il, L', La, Las, Le, Les, Lo, Los, M', Mac, Mc, O', Per, Saint, San, Santa, Santo, St., Ste., Te, Ten, Ter, Van, Van de, Van der, Von, Von der.

Study the following examples.

| NAME | KEY UNIT | ALPHABETIC FILING ORDER | | |
		UNIT 2	UNIT 3	UNIT 4
1. Oreste M. D'Acchille	DAcchille	Oreste	M	
2. Robt. K. D'Agostino	DAgostino	Robt	K	
3. D'alton Food Store	Dalton	Food	Store	
4. Ms. Beverly H. D'Amico	DAmico	Beverly	H	Ms
5. Jose Del Rio	DelRio	Jose		
6. Senator Paula DeYoung	DeYoung	Paula	Senator	
7. Doc LeRoy and Son	Doc	LeRoy	and	Son
8. Le Jo Roofing Co.	LeJo	Roofing	Co	
9. James P. Loo	Loo	James	P	
10. Marilyn J. Saint Clair	SaintClair	Marilyn	J	
11. San Jo Inn	SanJo	Inn		
12. San Jose Cab Co.	SanJose	Cab	Co	
13. Santa Fe Night Club	SantaFe	Night	Club	
14. Ms. Marilyn St. Clair	StClair	Marilyn	Ms	
15. Tony E. VanCamp	VanCamp	Tony	E	
16. Miss Wendy B. Van Camp	VanCamp	Wendy	B	Miss
17. Jessie N. Van Der Velde	VanDerVelde	Jessie	N	
18. Edwin F. VanDer Werff	VanDerWerff	Edwin	F	
19. Barnell VanDyke	VanDyke	Barnell		
20. Wesley O. Van Dyke	VanDyke	Wesley	O	

Rule 8 – Identical Names

When personal names and names of businesses, institutions, and organizations are identical, addresses determine the filing order. *Cities* are considered first, followed by *states* or *provinces, street names,* and *house numbers* or *building numbers,* in that order.

When the first units of street names are written as figures, file the names in ascending numeric order before alphabetic street names.

File street names with compass directions as written. File numbers appearing after compass directions before alphabetic names (East 8th, East Main, Sandusky, SE Eighth, Southeast Eighth).

File house or building numbers written as figures in ascending numeric order (9 Charter House, 417 Charter House) before alphabetic building names (The Charter House). If a street address and a building name are included in an address, disregard the building name. ZIP Codes are not considered in determining filing order.

Titles and suffixes are indexed according to Rule 5 and are considered *before* addresses.

Study the following examples.

ALPHABETIC FILING ORDER

NAME	KEY UNIT	UNIT 2	UNIT 3	ADDRESS
1. Elsie P. Franklin Bellingham, WA	Franklin	Elsie	P	Bellingham WA
2. Elsie P. Franklin Tacoma, WA	Franklin	Elsie	P	Tacoma WA
3. IGA Market Aurora, IL	IGA	Market		Aurora IL
4. Kings Dept. Store Aurora, IN	Kings	Dept	Store	Aurora IN
5. Kings Dept. Store Aurora, Ontario	Kings	Dept	Store	Aurora Ontario
6. McDonald's Restaurant 123 Beacon Ave. Houston, TX	McDonalds	Restaurant		Houston TX 123 Beacon Ave
7. McDonald's Restaurant 1019 Beacon Ave. Houston, TX	McDonalds	Restaurant		Houston TX 1019 Beacon Ave
8. McDonald's Restaurant 849 S. 24 St. Houston, TX	McDonalds	Restaurant		Houston TX 849 S 24 St
9. McDonald's Restaurant 241 SW 7 St. Houston, TX	McDonalds	Restaurant		Houston TX 241 SW 7 St
10. McDonald's Restaurant 1821 SW Tenth Houston, TX	McDonalds	Restaurant		Houston TX 1821 SW Tenth
11. McDonald's Restaurant 546 W. 22 St. Houston, TX	McDonalds	Restaurant		Houston TX 546 W 22 St
12. McDonald's Restaurant 81 World Bldg. Houston, TX	McDonalds	Restaurant		Houston TX 81 World Bldg

Name (Indexing Order)   Date

Instructions. Study page 17 before completing this exercise. Proceed as you did with previous indexing exercises. (1) Index and code each of the names in the list below. (2) Write the correct filing-order number in front of each name. (3) Write the names in correct alphabetic filing order in the space provided.

_____ Alexander K. DeFelice, Sr.
_____ Mrs. Camil Wilson LeRoy
_____ Mr. Camping International, Inc.
_____ St. Ann's Nursing Home
_____ LeRoux & Sons Garage
_____ Dominick Q. Defalco
_____ Raul Luis Majoros
_____ Mt. Carmel Cemetery

_____ Miss Maria I. DeFloria
_____ St. Ann's Rest Home
_____ Alexander K. DeFelice, Jr.
_____ Motor Rebuilders & Parts
_____ Kyoo H. Song
_____ Miss Antonette DeFalco
_____ Mountain Valley Water Co.
_____ Ms. Amy C. LeRoux

ALPHABETIC FILING ORDER

	KEY UNIT	UNIT 2	UNIT 3	UNIT 4
1.				
2.				
3.				
4.				
5.				
6.				
7.				
8.				
9.				
10.				
11.				
12.				
13.				
14.				
15.				
16.				

Name (Indexing Order)   Date

Instructions. Study pages 17 and 18 before completing this exercise. Proceed as you did with previous indexing exercises. (1) Index and code each of the names and addresses in the list below. (2) Write the correct filing-order number in front of each name. (3) Write the names in correct alphabetic filing order in the space provided.

_____ Ms. Laurie Mae Davis
Afton, WY

_____ First Natl. Bank
8025 Hill
Kansas City, MO

_____ Harry J. Foy, Jr.
Augusta, ME

_____ Alfanso O. Gonzales
256 NW Ninth
Atlanta, GA

_____ Ace Hardware
180 Harris
Cambridge, OH

_____ First Natl. Bank
520 Apple
Kansas City, MO

_____ Mrs. Laurie Mae Davis
Angola, IN

_____ First Natl. Bank
9920 Hill
Kansas City, MO

_____ Ace Hardware
1912 W. Alexis
Cambridge, MA

_____ Alfanso O. Gonzales
317 NW 5th St.
Atlanta, GA

_____ Miss Laurie Mae Davis
Detroit, MI

_____ Harry J. Foy, Sr.
Augusta, GA

_____ Ace Hardware
642 Main
Cambridge, MA

_____ First Natl. Bank
294 W. Brown
Kansas City, MO

ALPHABETIC FILING ORDER

	KEY UNIT	UNIT 2	UNIT 3	UNIT 4	ADDRESS
1.					
2.					
3.					
4.					
5.					
6.					
7.					
8.					
9.					
10.					
11.					
12.					
13.					
14.					

APPLICATION 3
Rules 5-8

Instructions. Proceed as you did with Application 1 (p. 9). Index, code, and file the cards in alphabetic order. List the numeric order of the correctly filed cards on a separate sheet of paper.

301

Dr. Taihe C. Okona

3155 Mozart Boulevard

Greenwood, MS 38930-8416

306

Doctor's Pharmacy

186 Ash Court

Elko, NV 89801-5048

302

National Steel Corp.

2551 Enid Road

Birmingham, AL 35201-3814

307

Mrs. Beverly Santa Rita

15 W. 6 Ave.

Murfreesboro, TN 37130-7816

303

Ms. Sue B. Mitchell

371 NE 74

Dayton, OH 45402-2640

308

National Steel Corp.

850 Ten Mile Rd.

Florence, AL 35630-6182

304

Arthur A. Long, Jr.

1329 Hunter Ct.

Butler, PA 16001-9864

309

Arthur A. Long II

503 Locust Rd.

Ocean City, MD 21842-3186

305

Miss Pennie E. LeVeck

629 Joyce Avenue

Kings Mountain, NC 28086-8042

310

Ms. Sue B. Mitchell

864 NE Second

Dayton, OH 45404-8431

APPLICATION 4
Rules 5-8

Instructions. Proceed as you did with Application 1 (p. 9). Index, code, and file the cards in alphabetic order. List the numeric order of the correctly filed cards on a separate sheet of paper.

401	406
Ms. Lena A. Madam 16 Scenic View Drive Bay Shore, NY 11706-4823	Mobile Glass Co. 236 W. 5th St. Mt. Vernon, OH 43050-8428

402	407
S. J. VonderBrink 38 Warren Ct. Towson, MD 21204-6812	Phillip C. Vonder Brink 714 Foust Ln. Portland, ME 04101-9126

403	408
Women Helping Women 6917 Dixie Hwy. Denver, CO 80203-3504	MR Burger Old State Road 27 Bristol, VA 24201-2018

404	409
Buero Vallejo 216 E. 6th Street Salem, OR 97301-2681	Madam's Beauty Nook 415 Oak Circle Woonsocket, RI 02895-0945

405	410
Miss Cathy M. Wood 461 Bowman Blvd. New Orleans, LA 70104-7926	Mobile Glass Co. 635 Elmore Rd. Midland, MI 48640-1689

APPLICATION 3
Rules 5-8

311

Ms. Pennie E. Le Veck

5614 Vogel Road

Barre, VT 05641-8631

316

Arthur A. Long III

4229 Georgia Drive

Harrisburg, AR 72432-1841

312

Doctor's Supply

560 Superior Avenue

Walla Walla, WA 99362-4811

317

Ms. Beverly Santos

346 Leslie Ave.

Derry, NH 03038-7621

313

National Steel Corp.

942 Elm St.

Anderson, IN 46011-5262

318

Arthur A. Long, Sr.

4457 Emerald Lane

Salem, NJ 08079-6438

314

Taihe C. Okona, D.D.S.

621 Ridge Ave.

Rapid City, SD 57701-3492

319

National Steel Corp.

640 Fifth St.

Anderson, SC 29621-3284

315

Ms. Sue B. Mitchell

217 Clark Rd.

Dayton, OH 45405-1867

320

Ms. Sue B. Mitchell

219 Clark Rd.

Dayton, OH 45405-1867

411

Scott G. Vonderbrink

8150 Mall Rd.

Murray, KY 42071-6741

416

Mobile Glass Co.

10542 Freemont Pike

Mt. Vernon, IL 62864-0186

412

Miss Catherine M. Wood

322 E. 17th Ave.

Norwalk, CT 06850-6214

417

Claudia E. Madams

625 W. 11th Street

Gallatin, TN 37066-2618

413

Mobile Glass Co.

1115 Vinol Road

Midland, Ontario MSW 1E4

418

Miss Catherine M. Wood

421 E. 17th Ave.

Norwalk, CT 06850-6214

414

K. Y. Wong

1082 Cross Lane

Phoenix, AZ 85005-8430

419

Kai Yan Wong

82 Linden Lane

St. Louis, MO 63103-3214

415

Women's Center

Highway 36

Tulsa, OK 74104-0274

420

Mobile Glass Co.

8972 W. 5th St.

Mt. Vernon, IN 47620-1620

Learning Objectives

After completing Part III, you will be able to:

1. Index and alphabetize numbers in business names.
2. Index and alphabetize names of organizations and institutions.
3. Index and alphabetize separated single words in business names.
4. Index and alphabetize hyphenated personal and business names.

Rule 9 – Numbers in Business Names

File *numbers spelled out* in a business name alphabetically as written. *Numbers written in digit form* are one unit. *Names with numbers written in digit form as the first unit* are filed in ascending order before alphabetic names. *Arabic numerals are filed before Roman numerals* (2, 3; II, III). *Names with inclusive numbers* (33-37) are arranged by the first number only (33). *Names with numbers appearing in other than the first position* (Pier 36 Cafe) are filed alphabetically within the appropriate section and immediately before a similar name without a number (Pier and Port Cafe).

When indexing numbers written in digit form that contain *st, d,* and *th* (1st, 2d, 3d, 4th), ignore the letter endings and consider the digits (1, 2, 3, 4).

Study the following examples. NOTE: All numbers in digit form precede all alphabetic names in a file.

	ALPHABETIC FILING ORDER			
NAME	KEY UNIT	UNIT 2	UNIT 3	UNIT 4
1. 2d and Rose Management	2	and	Rose	Management
2. 15-18 Shop	15	Shop		
3. 80 Star Air Freight	80	Star	Air	Freight
4. 580 Building	580	Building		
5. Andrew J. DuBois Company	Andrew	J	DuBois	Company
6. Fifty Five Motors	Fifty	Five	Motors	
7. Five Acres Truck Stop	Five	Acres	Truck	Stop
8. Five-Hundred Block Co.	FiveHundred	Block	Co	
9. Four Point Catering	Four	Point	Catering	
10. Route 511 Restaurant	Route	511	Restaurant	
11. Sisters III Catering Service	Sisters	III	Catering	Service
12. Sisters Biscuits & Chicken	Sisters	Biscuits	and	Chicken
13. Sixth Street Viaduct	Sixth	Street	Viaduct	
14. Suite 550 Answering Service	Suite	550	Answering	Service
15. Suite 590 Beauty Nook	Suite	590	Beauty	Nook
16. Twenty-Four-Hour Bakery	TwentyFourHour	Bakery		

Rule 10 – Organizations and Institutions

File banks and other financial institutions, clubs, colleges, hospitals, hotels, lodges, motels, museums, religious institutions, schools, unions, universities, and other organizations and institutions according to the names written on their letterheads. "The" used as the first word in these names is the last filing unit.

Study the following examples.

NAME	KEY UNIT	UNIT 2	UNIT 3	UNIT 4
1. American Red Cross	American	Red	Cross	
2. Ameritrust Company NA	Ameritrust	Company	NA	
3. Bel Air Hotel	Bel	Air	Hotel	
4. Bel-Air Motel	BelAir	Motel		
5. City Loan & Savings	City	Loan	and	Savings
6. City Savings & Loan	City	Savings	and	Loan
7. El Bethel Church Inc.	ElBethel	Church	Inc	
8. Fraternal Order of Eagles	Fraternal	Order	of	Eagles
9. The Garden Club Forum	Garden	Club	Forum	The
10. Grant High School	Grant	High	School	
11. Hospital Council of Virginia	Hospital	Council	of	Virginia
12. Hotel Sofitel	Hotel	Sofitel		
13. Mount Oliver Baptist Church	Mount	Oliver	Baptist	Church
14. Mt. Sinai Pentecostal Church	Mt	Sinai	Pentecostal	Church
15. Museum of Art	Museum	of	Art	
16. Museum of Natural History	Museum	of	Natural	History
17. The Ohio State University	Ohio	State	University	The
18. Seaman's Service Lounge	Seamans	Service	Lounge	
19. St. Charles Hospital	StCharles	Hospital		
20. University of Ohio	University	of	Ohio	

Name (Indexing Order)   Date

Instructions. Study page 25 before completing this exercise. Proceed as you did with previous indexing exercises. (1) Index and code each of the names in the list below. (2) Write the correct filing-order number in front of each name. (3) Write the names in correct alphabetic filing order in the space provided.

_____ Four Seasons Builders	_____ Al L. Floyd
_____ A. L. Floyd	_____ 420 Madison Ave. Bldg.
_____ Bay View Yacht Club	_____ Miss Vesta Decant
_____ Raul de Castro	_____ 4 Star Bookstore
_____ Ping Fan	_____ Mrs. Jas. Delph
_____ Fourth Ohio Area Council	_____ Four SQ Builders
_____ Abacus II Computers	_____ J. P. Abair
_____ 4011 Corp.	_____ Ms. Gabriele D'Emilio

ALPHABETIC FILING ORDER

	KEY UNIT	UNIT 2	UNIT 3	UNIT 4
1.				
2.				
3.				
4.				
5.				
6.				
7.				
8.				
9.				
10.				
11.				
12.				
13.				
14.				
15.				
16.				

Name (Indexing Order)   Date

Instructions. Study page 26 before completing this exercise. Proceed as you did with previous indexing exercises. (1) Index and code each of the names in the list below. (2) Write the correct filing-order number in front of each name. (3) Write the names in correct alphabetic filing order in the space provided.

_____ Thos. St. Julian, Jr.

_____ Trinity Medical Center

_____ Twentieth Oil & Gas

_____ Shiu Tse

_____ Mrs. D. K. St. John

_____ 7416 Gift Shop

_____ Ms. Donna May St. Johns

_____ 21st Century Health Spa

_____ Twenty Grand Club

_____ 776 Resort Hotel

_____ Miss Donna May St. Johns

_____ Seven Hills Service Station

_____ Thos. Bob St. Julian

_____ Salem United Methodist Church

_____ Luis Vivaneo

_____ Tom's Carry Out

ALPHABETIC FILING ORDER

	KEY UNIT	UNIT 2	UNIT 3	UNIT 4
1.				
2.				
3.				
4.				
5.				
6.				
7.				
8.				
9.				
10.				
11.				
12.				
13.				
14.				
15.				
16.				

Rule 11 – Separated Single Words

When a single word is separated into two or more parts in a business name, the parts are considered separate indexing units. If a name contains two compass directions separated by a space (South East Car Rental), each compass direction is a separate indexing unit. *Southeast* and *south-east* are considered single indexing units. Cross-reference if necessary. For example: South East SEE ALSO Southeast, South-East.

Study the following examples.

		ALPHABETIC FILING ORDER		
NAME	KEY UNIT	UNIT 2	UNIT 3	UNIT 4
1. Air Way Auto Parts	Air	Way	Auto	Parts
2. Airway Mobile Homes	Airway	Mobile	Homes	
3. All State Rental Services	All	State	Rental	Services
4. All Weather Window Co.	All	Weather	Window	Co
5. Kenneth Allan	Allan	Kenneth		
6. Carlene Allen	Allen	Carlene		
7. Walter 0. Allpach	Allpach	Walter	0	
8. Miss Gayle C. Allspaw	Allspaw	Gayle	C	Miss
9. Allstate Van Lines Inc.	Allstate	Van	Lines	Inc
10. Christine P. Martinez	Martinez	Christine	P	
11. Truc Ngyten	Ngyten	Truc		
12. North East Ins. Clinic	North	East	Ins	Clinic
13. North Side Apartments	North	Side	Apartments	
14. Ms. Theresa P. North	North	Theresa	P	Ms
15. North Western Distributors Inc.	North	Western	Distributors	Inc
16. Northeast Ins. Services	Northeast	Ins	Services	
17. Robert E. Northern	Northern	Robert	E	
18. Northern Steel Transport Co.	Northern	Steel	Transport	Co
19. Northern Technical Institute	Northern	Technical	Institute	
20. Northgate Service Center	Northgate	Service	Center	

Rule 12 – Hyphenated Names

A. Personal Names. Hyphenated personal names are one indexing unit and the hyphen is ignored. *Jones-Bennett* is a single indexing unit — *JonesBennett*.

B. Business Names. Hyphenated business and place names and coined business names are one indexing unit and the hyphen is ignored. *La-Z-Boy* is a single indexing unit — *LaZBoy*.

Study the following examples.

NAME	KEY UNIT	UNIT 2	UNIT 3	UNIT 4
1. Ad-O-Graphics Inc.	AdOGraphics	Inc		
2. Advest Bank, Hartford, CT	Advest	Bank	Hartford	CT
3. Judy C. Allen-Chappel	AllenChappel	Judy	C	
4. Dr. Carmen 0. Aznar	Aznar	Carmen	O	Dr
5. Bay State Cable Television	Bay	State	Cable	Television
6. Bayshore Lobster Express	Bayshore	Lobster	Express	
7. Bay-Shore Super Shuttle	BayShore	Super	Shuttle	
8. Baystate Eye Associates	Baystate	Eye	Associates	
9. Austin C. Burton-Watson	BurtonWatson	Austin	C	
10. Micro-Wave Oven Service	MicroWave	Oven	Service	
11. Mini Price Motor Inn	Mini	Price	Motor	Inn
12. Mini-Rate Car Rental	MiniRate	Car	Rental	
13. Young Sung Sung	Sung	Young	Sung	
14. Young-Deok Sung	Sung	YoungDeok		
15. Tilt-Or-Lift	TiltOrLift			
16. Trans World Airlines	Trans	World	Airlines	
17. Transport Tire Inc.	Transport	Tire	Inc	
18. Trans-Travel & Tours	TransTravel	and	Tours	
19. Ms. Elsie Trice	Trice	Elsie	Ms	
20. Tri-County Alfalfa Coop.	TriCounty	Alfalfa	Coop	

Name (Indexing Order)   Date

Instructions. Study page 29 before completing this exercise. Proceed as you did with previous indexing exercises. (1) Index and code each of the names in the list below. (2) Write the correct filing-order number in front of each name. (3) Write the names in correct alphabetic filing order in the space provided.

_____ Miss Karen A. Vulich   _____ Newbury Food Shops

_____ North Town Electronics   _____ Bay View Milling Co.

_____ Ninh Dinh Vu   _____ Southwest Neighborhood Facility

_____ Bayview Golf Course   _____ Mrs. C. H. Bayer

_____ Ms. Juanita W. Valera   _____ Northtowne Square

_____ New Light Baptist Church   _____ Baybrook Realty Co.

_____ Six Star Auto Sales   _____ South West Industries Inc.

_____ C. Howard Bayer   _____ Rev. Robt. H. New

ALPHABETIC FILING ORDER

	KEY UNIT	UNIT 2	UNIT 3	UNIT 4
1.				
2.				
3.				
4.				
5.				
6.				
7.				
8.				
9.				
10.				
11.				
12.				
13.				
14.				
15.				
16.				

■ **Indexing Exercise 12** _____ _____

Name (Indexing Order)   Date

Instructions. Study page 30 before completing this exercise. Proceed as you did with previous indexing exercises. (1) Index and code each of the names in the list below. (2) Write the correct filing-order number in front of each name. (3) Write the names in correct alphabetic filing order in the space provided.

_____ Air Way Heating Co.
_____ Phil-Cord Labs Inc.
_____ Chan K. Hahn
_____ Karon Harrison-Pepper
_____ All World Travel Inc.
_____ Ms. Melissa J. Harriss
_____ Airway Rent A Car
_____ Roto-Rooter Sewer Cleaning

_____ Air-Way Consumer Products
_____ Roberto Franco-Saenz
_____ All-State Tire Sales
_____ WETO Television
_____ Kathryn Harris-Troost
_____ P-H Enterprises
_____ The Wells-Bowen Co.
_____ Larry A. Rothrock, Atty.

ALPHABETIC FILING ORDER

	KEY UNIT	UNIT 2	UNIT 3	UNIT 4
1.				
2.				
3.				
4.				
5.				
6.				
7.				
8.				
9.				
10.				
11.				
12.				
13.				
14.				
15.				
16.				

Part III – Alphabetic Indexing Rules 9-12

APPLICATION 5
Rules 9-12

Instructions. Proceed as you did with previous applications. Index, code, and file the cards in alphabetic order. List the numeric order of the correctly filed cards on a separate sheet of paper.

501

Mini Vacations International

219 River Rd.

Rutland, VT 05701-0164

506

Mid American National Bank

301 W. Central Street

Toledo, OH 43601-2112

502

Safe Way Credit Union

5618 N. Summit

Morristown, TN 37814-2168

507

Second Source

1615 Laskey Rd.

Nashua, NH 03060-3214

503

2d National Bank Bldg.

432 Floyd St.

Columbia, SC 29201-4169

508

2400 Answering Service

548 Laguna Dr.

Atlantic City, NJ 08401-6186

504

Board of Mental Retardation

1810 N. 12th Ave.

Bristol, RI 02809-0921

509

San Marcus Treatment Center

500 N. 164th St.

Santa Fe, NM 87501-2186

505

100 Percent Klean

210 S. Main Street

Johnstown, PA 15901-6445

510

Mid-American Preferred Insurance

612 Dixie Lane

Lexington, KY 40507-4161

APPLICATION 6
Rules 9-12

Instructions. Proceed as you did with previous applications. Index, code, and file the cards in alphabetic order. List the numeric order of the correctly filed cards on a separate sheet of paper.

601

1040 Audit Service

8630 Winton Road

Salem, OR 97301-1320

602

6415 Shop

716 Reading Rd.

San Diego, CA 92101-6481

603

Century 21 American Realty

2944 Fairfield Avenue

Portland, OR 97208-2612

604

Rite-Way Barber Supplies

733 Elm Drive

Dallas, TX 75221-1641

605

Tax Information Center

343 Clark Road

Denver, CO 80201-5214

606

Jean Ann Smith-Kelsey

324 Mozart Lane

Idaho Falls, ID 83401-3684

607

Route 650 Auto Parts

608 Woodford Drive

El Paso, TX 79940-0981

608

Tri-State Clinic

218 Hickory Lane

Monterey, CA 93940-6214

609

Up-Right Scaffolds

929 S. Oak Street

Newton, IA 50208-4318

610

Rite-Now Container Corp.

2307 Cody Ave.

Topeka, KS 66601-2186

APPLICATION 5
Rules 9-12

511

One Discount Golf, Inc.

6115 Wyandotte Rd.

Fairmont, WV 26554-2184

516

Midam Sales Associates

700 W. Boundary

Macomb, IL 61455-0145

512

South Western Art Institute

2516 Airport Hwy.

Montgomery, AL 36104-6204

517

Southwest Missouri State University

1127 Champion St.

Springfield, MO 65801-8968

513

240 Marina

712 Phillips

Albany, NY 12201-3186

518

Santiago's Sports Club

1127 Kury Avenue

Tucson, AZ 85702-1641

514

Midamerican Corvette Supplies

612 Byrne Rd.

New Castle, IN 47362-4121

519

Mid-Con Industries

1000 Jackson Road

Battle Creek, MI 49016-2120

515

1 Day Courier

3815 Seiss Ave.

Hagerstown, MD 21740-3184

520

Soos Plumbing & Heating

915 Adams St.

Dover, DE 19901-6892

APPLICATION 6
Rules 9-12

611

Tax Deduction Co.

585 Belt Line Rd.

Boise, ID 83701-0384

616

Jos. R. Smith-Hibbard

825 Cook Road

Lewistown, MT 59457-4301

612

6 Love Tennis Shop

815 Link Dr.

Salt Lake City, UT 84101-3824

617

Rite Finance Co.

3247 Tyler Avenue

Miami, FL 33101-2648

613

Up-Beat Music Center

702 Green Hills Boulevard

Tulsa, OK 74101-1621

618

Ten Mile Museum

2824 Pueblo Road

Sioux Falls, SD 57101-1321

614

Century 21 Americrest Realty

610 W. Hwy. 303

Reno, NV 89501-1441

619

Ramus Health Club

705 Murdock Street

Augusta, ME 04330-9428

615

TaWaNa Imports

513 High Lane

Lincoln, NE 68501-1662

620

Six Mile House

4313 Travis Circle

Bellingham, WA 98225-2121

Learning Objectives

After completing Part IV, you will be able to:

1. Index and alphabetize compound personal and business names.
2. Index and alphabetize government names.

Rule 13 – Compound Names

A. Personal Names. When separated by a space, compound personal names are considered separate indexing units. *Mary Lea Gerson* is three units.

Although *St. John* is a compound name, *St.* (Saint) is a prefix and follows Rule 7, which considers it a single indexing unit.

B. Business Names. Compound business or place names with spaces between the parts of the names follow Rule 11, and the parts are considered separate units. *New Jersey* and *Mid America* are considered two indexing units each.

Study the following examples.

NAME	KEY UNIT	UNIT 2	UNIT 3	UNIT 4
1. Miss Rose Ann Daniels	Daniels	Rose	Ann	Miss
2. Weldon Jake Dennis	Dennis	Weldon	Jake	
3. Lady Bug Fashions	Lady	Bug	Fashions	
4. Lake Land College	Lake	Land	College	
5. Lakeland Sports Center	Lakeland	Sports	Center	
6. Po-Hee Lu	Lu	PoHee		
7. Miss Rose Mary Maddox	Maddox	Rose	Mary	Miss
8. Ronald J. Madison	Madison	Ronald	J	
9. Neiman-Marcus	NeimanMarcus			
10. Netco	Netco			
11. Milton A. Netter, Jr.	Netter	Milton	A	Jr
12. New Jersey Aluminum Co.	New	Jersey	Aluminum	Co
13. New Woman Medical Center	New	Woman	Medical	Center
14. The New York Times	New	York	Times	The
15. Newark Electronics Corp.	Newark	Electronics	Corp	
16. Dr. Ruth S. Newbanks	Newbanks	Ruth	S	Dr
17. New-Leaf Nursery	NewLeaf	Nursery		
18. P C Mart	P	C	Mart	
19. Manuel Luis Perez	Perez	Manuel	Luis	
20. Peter Pan Bus Lines	Peter	Pan	Bus	Lines

Rule 14 – Government Names

A. Federal. File the name of a federal government agency by the name of the government unit (United States Government) followed by the most distinctive name of the office, bureau, department, etc., as written (Internal Revenue Service). The words "Office of," "Department of," "Bureau of," etc., *if needed* for clarity and in the official name, are separate indexing units.

If "of" is not a part of the official name as written, it is not added.

B. State and Local. File the names of state, province, county, parish, city, town, township, and village governments/political divisions by their distinctive names. The words "State of," "County of," "City of," "Department of," etc., *if needed* for clarity and in the official name, are considered separate indexing units (Wisconsin/Transportation/Department/of).

C. Foreign. The distinctive English name is the first indexing unit for foreign government names. This is followed, *if needed* and in the official name, by the balance of the formal name of the government. Branches, departments, and divisions follow in order by their distinctive names. States, colonies, provinces, cities, and other divisions of foreign governments are filed by their distinctive or official names as spelled in English (Canada; Poland; France; Paris). Cross-reference the written foreign name to the English name, if necessary.

Study the following examples.

Name	Index Form of Name
Department of Human Services Columbus, Georgia (City Gov't)	Columbus 　Human Services Department of 　Columbus Georgia
Ministry of Education San Jose, Costa Rica	Costa Rica 　Education Ministry of 　San Jose Costa Rica
Ministry of Finance Republic of Iceland Reykjavik, Iceland	Iceland Republic of 　Finance Ministry of 　Reykjavik Iceland
Coordinator of School Transportation Department of Education Mason City, Illinois (City Gov't)	Mason City 　Education Department of 　School Transportation Coordinator of 　Mason City Illinois
Mason County Safety Department Havana, Illinois (County Gov't)	Mason County 　Safety Department 　Havana Illinois
National Weather Service U.S. Department of Commerce Cincinnati, Ohio (Federal Gov't)	United States Government 　Commerce Department of 　National Weather Service 　Cincinnati Ohio
Civil Rights Division Department of Justice Washington, DC (Federal Gov't)	United States Government 　Justice Department of 　Civil Rights Division 　Washington DC
Bureau of Labor Statistics U.S. Department of Labor Washington, DC (Federal Gov't)	United States Government 　Labor Department of 　Labor Statistics Bureau of 　Washington DC

■ **Indexing Exercise 13**

Name (Indexing Order)   Date

Instructions. Study page 37 before completing this exercise. Proceed as you did with previous indexing exercises. (1) Index and code each of the names in the list below. (2) Write the correct filing-order number in front of each name. (3) Write the names in correct alphabetic filing order in the space provided.

_____ Good Hope Hospital

_____ 4 S Distribution Center

_____ Yearn OK Yoon

_____ Winston C. Fournier

_____ John Paul Youree

_____ Ramon de la Cruz

_____ Ruth Ann Goodman, Atty.

_____ Lillie Mae Goodnight, CPA

_____ Dunham-Bush Industrial Equip.

_____ Gateway Travel

_____ New England Travel

_____ D & B Parts

_____ Rev. Barbara Young-Blaine

_____ Ruthann Goodman, MD

_____ Four-E Ranch House

_____ Your Party Store

ALPHABETIC FILING ORDER

	KEY UNIT	UNIT 2	UNIT 3	UNIT 4
1.				
2.				
3.				
4.				
5.				
6.				
7.				
8.				
9.				
10.				
11.				
12.				
13.				
14.				
15.				
16.				

Name (Indexing Order)   Date

Instructions. Study page 38 before completing this exercise. Proceed as you did with previous indexing exercises. (1) Index and code each of the names in the list below. (2) Write the correct filing-order number in front of each name. (3) Write the names in correct alphabetic filing order in the space provided.

_____ Tax Department
Village of Chatham
Ontario, Canada

_____ Department of Commerce
State of Kentucky
Lexington, Kentucky

_____ Department of Public Works
Kingsport, Tennessee

_____ Department of Labor
Bogota, Colombia

_____ Minister of Foreign Affairs
Wellington, New Zealand

_____ Division of Air Transportation
Department of Commerce
Santiago, Chile

_____ Cheshire County Water Works
Keene, New Hampshire

_____ Bureau of Land Management
U.S. Department of Commerce
Casper, Wyoming

_____ State Highway Patrol
Camden, New Jersey

_____ Center for Disease Control
U.S. Public Health Service

ALPHABETIC FILING ORDER

1. _____

_____

_____

_____

2. _____

_____

_____

_____

3. _____

_____

_____

_____

4. _____

_____

_____

_____

5. _____

_____

_____

_____

6. _____

_____

_____

_____

7. _____

_____

_____

_____

8. _____

_____

_____

_____

9. _____

_____

_____

_____

10. _____

_____

_____

_____

Instructions. Proceed as you did with previous applications. Index, code, and file cards in alphabetic order. List the numeric order of the correctly filed cards on a separate sheet of paper.

701

Minister of Justice

State of Maldonado

Rocha, Uruguay

702

Police Department

Henry County

Martinsville, VA 24112-8641

703

Homecare Medical Rental

Southland Shopping Center

Covington, KY 41011-5481

704

Jo Ann Fabrics

201 Morris Road

Cleveland, OH 44100-4614

705

Office of Inspector General

U.S. Veterans Administration

St. Louis, MO 63100-3214

706

Mr. Richard C. Newsom

2601 Stanton Lane

Hartland, VT 05048-2168

707

Mrs. Alonzo Newsome

710 Monroe Street

Manchester, VT 05254-6130

708

Boating Safety Program

U.S. Coast Guard

Seattle, WA 98100-4628

709

Mr. Lingde Hong

326 Fearing Way

Lancaster, PA 17600-3214

710

Board of Vocational Ed.

Ministry of Education

Helsinki, Finland

42

APPLICATION 8
Rules 13-14

Instructions. Proceed as you did with previous applications. Index, code, and file cards in alphabetic order. List the numeric order of the correctly filed cards on a separate sheet of paper.

801

Department of Transportation

Village of Dansville

Dansville, NY 14437-2044

802

Crime Victims Compensation Board

State of Oklahoma

Oklahoma City, OK 73105-2121

803

Department of Agriculture

State of Oklahoma

Oklahoma City, OK 73105-8823

804

Commission of Cable Television

State of New York

270 Broadway

New York, NY 10122-3241

805

Ms. Minna Rae Johnson

92 Riverside Plaza

Conrad, IA 50621-1277

806

Office of the Aging

Steuben County

Bath, NY 14810-7233

807

Ms. Minna Raye Johnson

28 Fredonia Street

Conrad, MT 59425-0115

808

U.S. Department of Justice

Tenth St. & Constitution Ave. NW

Washington, DC 20530-3663

809

Ms. Minna Rae Johnson

22 Fredonia Street

Conrad, MT 59425-0112

810

U.S. Bureau of Labor Statistics

441 G Street NW

Washington, DC 20212-0441

711

Home Care Medical Supplies

617 Adams Court

Topeka, KS 66600-1486

716

U.S. Marshall's Service

Department of Justice

Austin, TX 78700-0124

712

Jo Ann's Lady Bug

367 E. State Line

Racine, WI 53400-1869

717

New Fellowship Church

2115 Central Ave.

Anchorage, AK 99501-3214

713

Ms. Rita Mae Francisco

219 W. Wayne Blvd.

Ponce, PR 00731-8421

718

Department of Finance

Republic of France

Paris, France

714

Antitrust Division

U.S. Dept. of Justice

Helena, MT 59601-1486

719

Fairfield County Park Board

Norwalk, CT 06850-6431

715

New Era Real Estate

18 E. 4th Street

Muskegon, MI 49440-1326

720

Home-Care Health Services

106 W. 3d St.

Charlotte, NC 28200-5891

811

University of Wyoming

Box 3434, University Station

Laramie, WY 82071-3434

816

Ministry of Finance

Republic of Pakistan

812

Alex Johnson

22 West Main St.

Greenville, PA 16125-3721

817

U.S. Department of Defense

The Pentagon

Washington, DC 20301-0999

813

Wyoming Resources Corp.

Claydesta Tower East

Midland, TX 79705-2112

818

Alex Johnson

2020 Avenue D

Greenville, SC 29609-3771

814

U.S. Steel Corp.

130 Lincoln Avenue

Vandergrift, PA 15690-1210

819

John Ritter

Hwy 59

Albany, TX 76430-1099

815

Office of the Aging

Wyoming County

Courthouse Square

Tunkhannock, PA 18657-0024

820

John Ritter, Jr.

50 Rockline Rd.

Albany, NY 12237-2121

◼ PART V ~ CROSS-REFERENCING ◼

Learning Objectives

After completing Part V, you will be able to:

1. Determine when cross-referencing is helpful or necessary.
2. Prepare cross-references.
3. Alphabetize cross-referenced items.

Sometimes it is helpful or necessary to index a name in more than one way. Cross-referencing becomes necessary:
1. When the material to be filed contains a reference to more than one name or subject.
2. When the material to be filed might be asked for by more than one name or subject.

If the cross-reference is made in a correspondence file, a cross-reference sheet is prepared and placed in the proper correspondence folder. If the cross-reference is made in a card file, a cross-reference card is prepared and filed in the card file.

The original piece of correspondence or the original card is indexed and filed under the most important name or subject; the cross-reference is indexed and filed under the secondary name or subject.

When names are identical or similar in pronunciation but different in spelling, a SEE ALSO cross-reference should be made to each of the various spellings (Smith SEE ALSO Schmidt, Schmit, Smyth).

An *X* is used on the cross-reference to indicate that the sheet or card is a cross-reference rather than an original, and the word SEE is used to identify the name or title under which the original piece of correspondence or the original card is filed.

Several cross-references may be prepared for any one piece of original correspondence or any one original card. The extent of cross-referencing will depend to a large degree upon the knowledge and judgment of the records manager and the needs of the office. Cross-references should be prepared, however, for the following types of names. *(The examples are already in the correct indexed order with original filing order on the left and cross-references on the right.)*

1. **Unusual Personal Names.** Index unusual names (names in which given names and surnames may be confused) in the normal way, using the name appearing last as the surname. Cross-reference to the as-written name.

   Akita Akemi

   David Paul

   X   Akemi Akita
        SEE Akita Akemi

   X   Paul David
        SEE David Paul

2. **Acronyms and Abbreviations.** Index the acronym or abbreviation as one unit. Cross-reference to the full name of the company or organization.

   IBM

   MADD

   X   International Business Machines Corporation
        SEE IBM

   X   Mothers Against Drunk Driving
        SEE MADD

3. **Popular and Coined Company Names.** Index and file under the popular or coined name. Cross-reference to the official company name.

   Joes

   River Cafe

   X   Joes Steak and Shake
        SEE Joes

   X   Bennetts River Cafe
        SEE River Cafe

4. Alternate Names. Index and file a married woman's name as she writes it. Cross-reference to other forms of her name to simplify finding material related to one person.

Lee Joan Snyder Mrs	X	Lee John R Mrs SEE Lee Joan Snyder Mrs
Guchi John *(John Yamaguchi uses the business name John Guchi)*	X	Yamaguchi John SEE Guchi John

5. Hyphenated Personal and Business Names. Index and file using the first name of a hyphenated name. Prepare a cross-reference for the second name.

BishopJones Carol H Mrs	X	Jones Carol H Bishop Mrs SEE BishopJones Carol H Mrs
StewartWarner Mfg Co	X	WarnerStewart Mfg Co SEE StewartWarner Mfg Co

6. Foreign Business Names. Index and file under the translated name and cross-reference to the foreign name.

Joy Manufacturing Company of France	X	Compagnie Joy S A SEE Joy Manufacturing Company of France

7. Foreign Government Names. Index and file under the translated name and cross-reference to the foreign name.

Equador Republic of Education Secretary of	X	Republica Oriental del Equador Secretario de Education SEE Equador Republic of Education Secretary of

8. Compound Names. Index and file under the first surname of a firm name containing the names of two or more individuals. Cross-reference to all other surnames in the firm name.

Doyle Lewis and Warner Associates	X	Lewis Warner and Doyle Associates SEE Doyle Lewis and Warner Associates
	X	Warner Doyle and Lewis Associates SEE Doyle Lewis and Warner Associates

9. Changed Names. When the name of an organization, publication, or individual is changed, index and file under the new name and cross-reference to the former name.

US Air Formerly Allegheny Airlines	X	Allegheny Airlines SEE US Air

10. Divisions or Subsidiaries. Index and file under the division or subsidiary name. Cross-reference to the parent company name.

Radio Shack	X	Tandy Corporation SEE Radio Shack

11. Names with Separated Single Words. A SEE ALSO cross-reference is prepared for names that may be written as one or two words.

North West Properties, Inc.	X	Northwest SEE ALSO North West, North-West

12. Similar Names. Surnames may be similar in pronunciation but different in spelling. SEE ALSO cross-references are made to the various spellings of the name.

Brown Joe	X	Browne SEE ALSO Braun Brown
	X	Braun SEE ALSO Brown Browne
	X	Brown SEE ALSO Browne Braun

Name (Indexing Order)　　　　　　　Date

Instructions. Study pages 45 and 46 before completing this exercise. Underline the first indexing unit of the original name and the first indexing unit of the cross-referenced name. Place an *X* beside the cross-referenced name. In the space provided, write the cross-referenced name or names first (preceded by an *X*); then indicate the original name under which the material is filed by writing that name on the next line preceded by the word *SEE*. *The first one has been completed as an example.*

1. The magazine <u>WILDERNESS</u> CAMPING ^X

   changed to <u>BACKPACKER</u>

   1. x <u>WILDERNESS</u> CAMPING

      SEE BACKPACKER

2. The name of Southern Airlines was changed to Republic Airlines

   2. _____

      _____

3. Nut Hut is a popular name for Tropical Nut Hut

   3. _____

      _____

      _____

4. Leatherman, Witzler & DeCessna, Attorneys

   4. _____

      _____

      _____

      _____

      _____

      _____

5. Sohio (Standard Oil of Ohio)

   5. _____

      _____

6. Aerolineas Argentinas is the foreign spelling of Argentina Airlines

   6. _____

      _____

7. Bell may also be spelled Belle

   7. _____

      _____

8. 3M (Minnesota Mining & Mfg. Co.)

   8. _____

      _____

9. Thomas Donald

   9. _____

      _____

10. Southside is also spelled South Side

    10. _____

        _____

11. Scripps-Howard Broadcasting

    11. _____

        _____

12. Mr. Teng Kim

    12. _____

        _____

13. Murphy's Mart is a Division of Ames Dept. Stores

    13. _____

        _____

14. Mrs. Lonetta Sue Hodges is also Mrs. Gordon Hodges

    14. _____

        _____

Name (Indexing Order)   Date

Instructions. (1) Code each of the names in the list below. The names are in indexing order. (2) Write the correct alphabetic order number in front of each name and cross-reference (1-28). (3) Write the names and the cross-references in correct alphabetic indexing order on the lines provided at the right.

Indexing Order	Alphabetic Order
_____ U S Steel Corporation	_____
_____ SEE USX	_____
_____ Frischs Restaurants	_____
_____ SEE Big Boy	_____
_____ Herold Mary James Mrs	_____
_____ SEE JamesHerold Mary Mrs	_____
_____ Chien Wang	_____
_____ SEE Wang Chien	_____
_____ Low	_____
_____ SEE ALSO Lowe	_____
_____ Federated Department Stores	_____
_____ SEE Lazarus	_____
_____ American Telephone and Telegraph	_____
_____ SEE ATandT	_____
_____ Gulf and Western Inc	_____
_____ SEE Paramount Pictures	_____
_____ BoneyHines Alison	_____
_____ SEE Hines Alison Boney	_____
_____ Petroleos deVenezuela	_____
_____ SEE Venezuela Oil Corp	_____
_____ Tractor Supply Co	_____
_____ SEE TSC	_____
_____ Ash Moodie Miss	_____
_____ SEE Boshart Moodie Mrs	_____
_____ South Western	_____
_____ SEE ALSO Southwestern	_____
_____ Shipley and Lodge Assoc.	_____
_____ SEE Lodge and Shipley Assoc.	_____

Learning Objectives

After completing Part VI, you will be able to:

1. Code and arrange names and subjects in alphabetic order in a subject file.
2. Code and arrange names in numeric order.
3. Code and arrange names in a geographic file.

SUBJECT FILING. Subject filing is the arrangement of records by the subject of the records. Filing by the subject of the correspondence rather than by the name of the correspondent is most feasible when the subject will provide quicker or easier access to the records. A subject file brings together all papers relating to a specific person, activity, date, or other topic.

Arrangement of a subject file should be functional—by business functions, by departments, or by whatever topics will provide the information quickly. Functional subjects may be accounting, administration, marketing, and so forth. A company that files records by departments may have accounting, marketing, and personnel departments.

A piece of correspondence is coded first by its subject and then by the name of the correspondent. If the subject does not appear in the correspondence, it is written in the upper right corner and coded. Some records personnel always write the subjects on the records for quicker identification. Coding the subject in the correspondence or writing it on the correspondence are both acceptable methods. (See page 50.) Subjects may be abbreviated to save space.

If a record may be requested by more than one subject, a cross-reference sheet is prepared or a photocopy of the original record is made and filed in the alternative subject folder. The cross-reference is marked on the original record with an *X* in the margin and a wavy underline. (See page 50.)

Study the following examples.

		ALPHABETIC FILING ORDER		
KEY UNIT	**UNIT 2**	**UNIT 3**	**UNIT 4**	**UNIT 5**

A company may file the names of its advertising contacts under the type of advertising media the contact represents.

Advertising	Aerial	Eagle	Air	Inc
	Agencies	Academy	Art	Studio
	Newspaper	Catholic	Chronicle	
	Radio	American	Sound	Productions
		WCWA	Radio	Station

An insurance company may file the names of its policyholders under the type of insurance policy.

Auto	Miller	James	F	Mr
	Miller	Lawrence	K	Dr
Homeowner	Oneil	Nichole	K	Ms
	ONeill	Ocelia	T	Miss
Life	Cheng	Teresa	F	Miss
Marine	Padon	Robert		
	Padone	Cliff	D	

Eastern Department Store

136 East Superior Street
Albany, NY 12206-3248
(518) 672-8690

April 1, XXXX

6 4 5 3
Ms. /Helen/M./Simpson
1622 E. Walnut
Cleveland, OH 44106-0982

Dear Ms. Simpson:

Your application for a <u>Credit</u>/Account with Eastern has been approved.
                         2

Your credit card has been sent to our Cleveland store. Please visit
the credit office in our <u>Cleveland store</u> located at 65 East Front in
downtown Cleveland and receive your credit card. The credit manager
will explain the simple procedures necessary for you to follow in
using your card.

If you have questions at any time, please call or write this office.
Of course, you are most welcome to visit our Cleveland credit office
for answers about our convenient services.

Thank you for your application for credit. We hope you will visit
our stores and use your credit card frequently.

Cordially yours,

Jane E. Smith

Jane E. Smith
Credit Manager

jkm

                                    x Credit
                                         1
                                      Account
                                         2

Letter Coded for Subject Filing

SIC Superior Insurance Company
16 North Allway
San Francisco, CA 94106-3428

                                              Insurance
                                                 Mobile
                                                    2
                                May 15, XXXX

5   4   3
Mr. /Juan/Ortega
156 South 18 St.
Modesto, CA 95350-6138

Dear Mr. Ortega:

We want to give immediate attention to any claim relating to your
mobile home policy.

It will speed up the processing of a claim if you will answer
the questions on the enclosed stamped, addressed card and send it
to us as soon as possible. Or if you wish, you may telephone us
at 415-372-6541. Please have the card with the completed answers
available. This will help us process your claim quickly.

If you need additional information, please write or call.

                        Sincerely,

                        Robert R. Johnson

                        Robert R. Johnson
                        Claims Adjuster

rcm

Enclosure

Letter Coded for Subject Filing

CROSS-REFERENCE SHEET

Name or Subject *Credit Account*
Cleveland Store

Date of Item *4/1/XXXX*

Regarding *Application for credit*

SEE

Name or Subject *Credit Account*
Simpson Helen M Ms

Authorized by *J. K. J.* Date *4/3/XXXX*

Cross-Reference Sheet for Letter (top left)

NUMERIC FILING. Numeric filing consists of arranging records in order by number. Information filed numerically is found quickly because numbers are in a definite order. An alphabetic filing system requires that a person remember that *p* comes after *o, e* comes after *d,* etc.

The use of a numeric system requires that each name or subject be assigned a number. An accession book is used for assigning new numbers. The accession book is filled with numbered blank lines. When a new file is created, the next available number is assigned, and the name of the file is written on the blank line in the accession book in as-written order. Then the name is added to an alphabetic index, a card file or computer file of all correspondent names or subject titles arranged alphabetically. The number assigned to the name is placed beside the name. (See page 52.)

To locate a file, you look for the name or subject in the alphabetic index. The number beside the name will direct you to the numeric file where you will find the file you want. A person using a numeric file frequently will soon remember many of the numbered files and will save time by lack of need to refer to the alphabetic index.

To save filing space, it is advisable to use a general alphabetic folder (A, M, S, etc.) to file information until the volume of material is sufficient to justify creating a specific numeric file for a person, company, or subject.

Advantages of numeric filing include (1) a folder with a number can be located faster and easier than an alphabetic folder; (2) cross-references are not needed in the numbered file because they are part of the alphabetic card file; (3) numbers afford some privacy because it is difficult to relate a number to a name without access to the alphabetic card file; and (4) a numeric filing system can be expanded without limit because there is always another number.

Disadvantages of numeric filing to consider are (1) the time necessary to consult the alphabetic index to determine the numeric file number; (2) misfiled papers are more difficult to locate when an incorrect number has been used; and (3) the exact order of digits in a number is more difficult to remember than the order of letters in a word.

A consecutive numeric filing system is ideal for medical records, insurance policies, bank accounts, drivers' licenses, charge accounts, replacement parts, student records, and social security records.

NUMERIC SUBJECT FILING. Assigning a number to each subject in a filing system permits a filing system to be adapted to computer processing and helps individuals using the system file retrieve information quickly. For example, if the number *311* is assigned to insurance, all individuals would consult the numeric chart of accounts and file or retrieve information about insurance using number *311.*

Consecutive Numeric File
Accession Book

Number	Name	Date
1561	Wells Supply Co.	May 1, XXXX
1562	Robert T. Fulton	May 1, XXXX
1563	Bonnie M. Jamison	May 2, XXXX
1564	Pablo Galvez	May 2, XXXX
1565	Swee-Heng Tan	May 3, XXXX

Alphabetic Index

Fulton Robert T 1562
Galvez Pablo 1564
Jamison Bonnie M. 1563
Tan SweeHeng 1565
Wells Supply Co 1561

Numeric Subject File
Business Expenses

301	Advertising	312	Office Supplies
303	Cleaning	313	Payroll Tax
304	Delivery	315	Rent
305	Electricity	317	Repairs
307	Heating	318	Salaries
311	Insurance	320	Telephone

Number	Activity
318	Issued payroll checks
304	Paid UPS
315	Signed building lease
320	Called branch office
311	Purchased liability policy

SMITH MACHINE and WELDING

599 Plaza Drive
Plymouth, MA 02360-6321

January 31, XXXX

3 2
Ms./Bernice/Fisher
5011 SR 23
Beloit, WI 53511-2681

Dear Ms. Fisher:

We have just completed an audit of our accounts receivable.
The information contained in your account indicates that $150 was
due from you on January 15, 19--.

If you have mailed your check, please disregard this letter.
If the account is still unpaid, please pay it as soon as possible.

We appreciate your business and invite you to send us additional
orders.

Yours truly,

Rex Lowe

Rex Lowe
Auditor

pkb

Letter Coded for Numeric Filing

Accession Book

Number	Name	Date
111	Mr. Mark Chang	Feb. 3, XXXX
112	Ms. Bernice Fisher	Feb. 3, XXXX
113	Dan s Mfg. Co.	Feb. 4, XXXX
114		
115		

Computer Alphabetic Index

Name	File No.
Chang Mark Mr	111
Dan s Mfg Co	113
Fisher Bernice Ms	112

Alphabetic Card File

Fisher Bernice Ms   112

Ms. Bernice Fisher
5011 SR 23
Beloit, WI 53511-2681

GEOGRAPHIC FILING. Geographic filing consists of arranging records alphabetically by geographic location of an individual, an organization, or a project. Geographic locations may be categorized by countries, states, cities, regions of the country, regions of the state, or by street names. A geographic filing system is used when the nature of the business is related more to locations than to names of persons or companies. (See page 54, *Letter Coded for Geographic Filing.*)

Organizations such as clubs, unions, fraternities, sororities, and professional groups use geographic filing to locate a member's name quickly. Businesses with customers residing across the United States or all over the world use geographic filing.

Consider how quickly you could locate a name when it is filed geographically by city as compared with looking at all the names spelled a particular way in the United States or in the world.

For ease in locating records in a geographic file, it is necessary to maintain an alphabetic index.

The two basic arrangements of geographic filing systems are *dictionary* and *encyclopedic.*

The dictionary geographic file consists of one alphabetic arrangement (A to Z) of geographic locations. For example, a filing system with folders for all the cities in a state or all the states in the United States arranged from A to Z would be an effective geographic filing system, with a few hundred or perhaps a few thousand names.

The encyclopedic arrangement is the alphabetic arrangement of major geographic divisions plus one or more geographic subdivisions also arranged in alphabetic order. For example, a filing system with folders for all the cities in a state arranged from A to Z and with folders in each city arranged from A to Z.

Study the following example of a geographic file with names listed alphabetically within the geographic locations of states and cities.

STATE	CITY	KEY UNIT	UNIT 2	UNIT 3	UNIT 4
MS	Biloxi	Chandler	Laura	C	Ms
		Chaney	Lowell	A	Jr
	Vicksburg	Chang	Cheng	Fu	
NH	Dover	Guarantee	Financial	Inc	
	Nashua	Morrison	Packaging	Co	
	Portsmouth	Guarrero	Emilena		
SC	Greenwood	Aleman	Daniel	Jr	
		Aleman	Danl	G	Rev
TN	Memphis	Key	Tronic	Corp	
		Oil	City	Petroleum	
	Nashville	McGhee	Darryl		
UT	Sandy	Perky	Loretta	Miss	
	Vernal	Shindler	Elyn	J	
VA	Norfolk	Messenger	Dewayne		
		Williams	Minnie	Lee	Miss
	Portsmouth	Peters	Billee	0	
WV	Clarksburg	G	W	C	Corp
		Inco	Ltd		
	Huntington	King	Felicia	K	Mrs

Future/Computer/Systems
114 North Terrace
2 (Helena,) (MT) 59601-0672

October 1, XXXX

Ms. Dawn C. Wingate
Micro Computer Services
489 Jackman Road
Great Falls, MT 59401-0134

Dear Ms. Wingate:

Thank you for your recent inquiry about our new double-coated ribbons.

These ribbons will provide consistently clearer copies and will give you at
least twice as much service as regular single-coated ribbons. Additional
information about the new double-coated ribbons is enclosed.

For your convenience, we have asked our (Great Falls,) (Montana,) representative,
Electronic /Data /Associates, to contact you. They will be able to provide you
with instant service. In addition, you will save shipping charges from Helena
on your orders.

If we can provide you with additional information or be of service to you in
any way, just call 406-497-6321.

Sincerely,

Beatrice Pulver

Beatrice Pulver
Vice President/Sales

mlg

Enclosure

Letter Coded for Geographic Filing

■ **Indexing Exercise 17** _____ _____

Name (Indexing Order)   Date

Subject Filing Instructions. Study page 49 before completing this exercise. (1) Code each of the names in the list below by subject and then by name. (2) Write the correct filing-order number in front of each subject and name. (3) Write the names and subjects in correct alphabetic filing order in the space provided. Abbreviated codes for accounts: Checking – CK, Home Loan – HL, Individual Retirement Account – IRA, Savings – SVG, Trust – TR.

_____ Dr. Pete Louis Kilroy, IRA

_____ Willis Rick Samson, HL

_____ Ms. Mary Jo Kimmel, SVG

_____ Floyd W. Kindall, Sr., TR

_____ Tyrone R. Kimbel, Atty., IRA

_____ Duke P. Salisbury, CK

_____ Gordon J. Kimble, SVG

_____ E. Burke Samuelson, Jr., HL

_____ Rhonda Beth Samuels, HL

_____ Ms. Kathleen Ann Salkin, CK

_____ Kyoo H. Kim, IRA

_____ Laura Mary Kimberly, SVG

_____ Kristi Jo Kimple, SVG

_____ Clairenne May Kindel, TR

_____ Miss Joaquin Oliva Salinas, CK

_____ Tony Edward Sanborn, TR

ALPHABETIC FILING ORDER BY SUBJECTS

	KEY UNIT	UNIT 2	UNIT 3	UNIT 4	UNIT 5
1.					
2.					
3.					
4.					
5.					
6.					
7.					
8.					
9.					
10.					
11.					
12.					
13.					
14.					
15.					
16.					

Part VI – Other Filing Methods   55

■ **Indexing Exercise 18** _____ _____

Name (Indexing Order)   Date

Numeric Filing Instructions. Study pages 51 and 52 before completing this exercise. (1) Code each of the names in the list below. (2) Write each of the names in the accession book in order of the date the account was established. Use the current year. (3) Write the names in correct alphabetic and indexing order with assigned numbers in the alphabetic index.

Accession Book

Number	Name	Date
1574		
1575		
1576		
1577		
1578		
1579		
1580		
1581		
1582		
1583		

Assigned Number

_____ Robert M. Mac Quigg, May 18, XXXX

_____ Salvador Ayson, May 7, XXXX

_____ Miss Molinda Adair, May 12, XXXX

_____ Advanced Mfg. Systems, May 21, XXXX

_____ Mary Kay Cosmetics, May 15, XXXX

_____ 760 Travel, Inc., May 9, XXXX

_____ Caroline Avery-Dahl, May 16, XXXX

_____ Ms. Louise A. Lindell, May 11, XXXX

_____ National Business Systems, May 5, XXXX

_____ Charles M. Neal, Sr., May 20, XXXX

FILING ORDER OF ALPHABETIC INDEX

	KEY UNIT	UNIT 2	UNIT 3	UNIT 4	NUMERIC
1.					
2.					
3.					
4.					
5.					
6.					
7.					
8.					
9.					
10.					

Name (Indexing Order)   Date

Geographic Filing Instructions. Study page 53 before completing this exercise. (1) Code each of the names in the list below first by the state and then by the city. (2) Code the individual or business name. (3) Write the correct filing-order number in front of each geographic location and name. (4) Write the states, cities, and names in correct geographic filing order in the spaces provided.

_____ McDowell Enterprises, Salem, AR

_____ Cathy M. Quimby, Medford, OR

_____ Travis C. Misso, Bellingham, WA

_____ Edgar R. Erback, Salem, OR

_____ Annie E. Horton, Cheyenne, WY

_____ Kerr-Addison Mines, Ltd., Waterville, WA

_____ Joyce W. Goodnight, Warren, AR

_____ Elaine B. Mackie, Bellingham, WA

_____ Chunfu T. Qui, Medford, NM

_____ Guilford Hotel, Rawlins, WY

_____ G.R.I. Corp., Rawlins, WY

_____ Equity Income Fund, Salem, OR

_____ Carles Recardo, Little Rock, AR

_____ Mission West Prop., Bellingham, WA

_____ Alice Rector, Little Rock, AR

_____ Ben J. Horton, Cheyenne, WY

GEOGRAPHIC FILING ORDER

	KEY UNIT	UNIT 2	UNIT 3	UNIT 4	UNIT 5
1.					
2.					
3.					
4.					
5.					
6.					
7.					
8.					
9.					
10.					
11.					
12.					
13.					
14.					
15.					
16.					

■ **Indexing Exercise 20**

Name (Indexing Order)   Date

Geographic Filing Instructions. Study page 53 before completing this exercise. (1) Code each of the names in the list below first by the state and then by the city. (2) Code the individual or business name. (3) Write the correct filing-order number in front of each geographic location and name. (4) Write the states, cities, and names in correct geographic filing order in the spaces provided.

_____ Computer Land, Inc., Springfield, IL
_____ John Powers Electronics, Rochester, MT
_____ Portland Cement Co., Portland, OR
_____ Wilkes Tree Farm, Newark, DE
_____ Beverly C. Monroe, Rochester, MT
_____ Electric City, Inc., Atlanta, GA
_____ Abba D Plumbing, Springfield, MO
_____ Cerre Ceramic Studios, Atlanta, GA

_____ Toby's Tack Shop, Newark, DE
_____ City Office Supplies, Rochester, MI
_____ City College, Savannah, GA
_____ Amy's Sports Center, Honolulu, HI
_____ Genesis Cinema, Jackson, MS
_____ Computer Magic, Springfield, MA
_____ Computer Magic, Conrad, MT
_____ The Computer Store, Conrad, MT

GEOGRAPHIC FILING ORDER

	KEY UNIT	UNIT 2	UNIT 3	UNIT 4	UNIT 5
1.					
2.					
3.					
4.					
5.					
6.					
7.					
8.					
9.					
10.					
11.					
12.					
13.					
14.					
15.					
16.					

Part VI – Other Filing Methods

Name (Indexing Order)   Date

Instructions. Study all rules before completing this exercise. The purpose of this exercise is to provide practice in interfiling records. The names listed on this page are to be interfiled with the list of names on page 60. (1) Code each of the names in the list below. (2) For each name in the list, determine the name in the list of names on page 60 that should immediately precede the name you are considering. (3) Write the number of the name that you have selected from the list on page 60 in front of the name on this page.

_____ Frame-It

_____ Mrs. Lenora Ealy

_____ Dr. B. Kevin Folsom

_____ Roberto Franco-Saenz

_____ Mr. Kevin Fitzpatrick

_____ Miss Mittie Mae Fulbright

_____ Fibronics International

_____ Herbert K. Fabian, Jr.

_____ Mrs. Jeanine Haber

_____ Andrea E. Freeman

_____ Joseph Farnell, CPA

_____ Charla K. Easlon

_____ Miss Deanna Halstead

_____ Jo Anne Fozman

_____ Jack E. Eaker II

_____ John W. Eberline

_____ El Shaddai Tours

_____ GAF Corp.

_____ 800 Bookstore

_____ Forty-Four Wall Street Fund

_____ Ms. Adrian Earnst

_____ David Q. Fivel

_____ Ms. Joni Galetka

_____ Peggy D. Elder-Moore

_____ Clifford T. Fagan

_____ Ministry of State
Kingdom of Ethiopia

_____ Eastman Kodak

_____ Sunsang Fung

_____ Ernest E. Gateson III

_____ 8758 Photo Shop

_____ Gallery of Flowers

_____ Jose P. Garcia

_____ Ful-Vue Display Systems

_____ Miss Nellie R. Forgaty

_____ Mrs. Ava B. Friberg

_____ East Coast Credit

_____ Mr. Bret Gaston

_____ Ms. Helen Grey Eaton

_____ Eastern Michigan University

_____ Paula Fisette-Sueeney

_____ Roger A. Harper, D.D.S.

_____ Ford Motor Corp.

_____ Four Star Tennis Academy

_____ Wing Cheung Hahn

_____ Galaxy Carpet Mills

_____ Marvene C. Easterly

_____ HAL, Inc.

_____ Lucas P. Francia

_____ H. Mathews Garman

_____ Future Electronics

■ **Indexing Exercise 21 (cont.)** _____ _____

Instructions. Follow the instructions on page 59. The names listed below are in correct indexing and alphabetic order. Coding is not necessary but may be done if you find it helpful when interfiling the two lists of names. The numbers are for your convenience in interfiling the names on page 59 with the list of names below.

1. 525 Club	46. Four S Ranch
2. 4210 Montrose Motors	47. Foys Garage
E 3. E and E Catering Services	48. Foyt Chevrolet Inc
4. Eagan Lewis G Mrs	49. Frame Corner The
5. Eagleson W F Miss	50. Frame David Sr
6. Eakin Gerald	51. France Republic Trade Dept
7. Earl Nora Lee	52. Frances Beatrice
8. Early Natalie F CPA	53. Franceschi Antonio J
9. Easley Ray K Sr	54. Francis B N Mrs
10. East Cab Company	55. Freed DeBow
11. East Gilbert L Col	56. Friar Tucks Antiques
12. East Side Sand Company	57. Fuentes Domingo Arroyo
13. Easter Seal Society	58. Fuji Electric Corporation
14. Eastern Kentucky University	59. FullerAustin Insulation Company
15. Eastlake Elementary School	60. Fung Sokyee
16. Eastwood Susie	61. FuTrek Business Computer Systems
17. Eberhart Opal	G 62. Gabaldon Manuel
18. EJs Carpet and Upholstery	63. Gaddis May Bell
19. ElAmin Florence	64. GaidoLingle Company Inc
20. ElChico Restaurant	65. Galbraith Fred H Maj
21. Elmi Hadi	66. Gale H Douglas
22. Emils Polo Club	67. Galena Park City Police Dept
23. Episcopal Church East Denver	68. Galena Park Elementary School
F 24. F and C Barber Shop	69. Galleria Plaza Hotel
25. FabCon Limited	70. Galveston South West Realty
26. Fabios Foreign Car Service	71. Ganatra Madhusudan
27. Factor Helen	72. Garlutzos Dance Studio
28. Farmers Insurance Group	73. Garrett Mable Dr
29. Federal Housing Administration	74. Garuda Indonesian Airlines
SEE United States Government	75. Gaslite Motel
Department of Housing	76. Gates Stephen C
and Urban Development	77. GatesStone and Company
30. FidelitySouthern Insurance Co	H 78. H C I Chemicals USA
31. Fifth Wheel The	79. Haanstads Camera Store
32. Fish Esther 0	80. Haas Lulu
33. Fishers Auto Parts	81. Hackethal Clement R II
34. Fishman Debby	82. Hair by Louis
35. Fitzcharles William N	83. Hakala Joseph M DDS
36. Fitzgerald Audrey M Mrs	84. Halcyon The Weavers Friend
37. FitzGerald Joseph E	85. HangUps for the Home
38. FitzSimmons and Company	
39. Fivecoat Robert	
40. FiveP Ektachrome Laboratory	
41. Flakt Incorporated Marine Div	
42. Fondren Elma Fay Mrs	
43. Forest Cindy K	
44. Fort Bend County Auditors Office	
45. Fort Spriggs Club	